good news, great joy

DEVOTIONS FOR ADVENT & CHRISTMAS
2024–2025

D1713284

AUGSBURG FORTRESS

Minneapolis

GOOD NEWS, GREAT JOY

Devotions for Advent & Christmas 2024–2025

References to ELW are from *Evangelical Lutheran Worship*, copyright © 2006 Evangelical Lutheran Church in America.

References to ACS are from *All Creation Sings*, copyright © 2020 Augsburg Fortress.

Quotations from the book of Psalms are from *ELW*. All other scripture quotations are from the New Revised Standard Version Bible, copyright © 1989 by the Division of Christian Education of the National Council of the Churches of Christ in the USA. Used by permission. All rights reserved.

"Household blessings and prayers" are from *Bread for the Day 2024: Daily Bible Readings and Prayers*, copyright © 2023 Augsburg Fortress.

pISBN 979-8-8898-3369-7
eISBN 979-8-8898-3379-6

Writers: Michael Coffey (December 1–7), Priscilla Austin (December 8–9, 19–21), Troy M. Troftgruben (December 10–18), Annabelle Peake Markey (December 22–28), Dena Williams (December 29–January 2), Felix Malpica (January 3–6)

Editor: Laurie J. Hanson
Cover design: Alisha Lofgren
Cover and interior images: All images © Getty Images. Used by permission.
Interior design and typesetting: Eileen Engebretson

Manufactured in China.

Welcome

In that region there were shepherds living in the fields, keeping watch over their flock by night. Then an angel of the Lord stood before them, and the glory of the Lord shone around them, and they were terrified. But the angel said to them, "Do not be afraid; for see—I am bringing you good news of great joy for all the people: to you is born this day in the city of David a Savior, who is the Messiah, the Lord. This will be a sign for you: you will find a child wrapped in bands of cloth and lying in a manger."—Luke 2:8-12

An angel came to some shepherds watching their sheep one night. That would have been surprising, to say the least! Then the angel announced not just good news but *good news of great joy*, and not just for the shepherds but for *all people*: Jesus, the Messiah and Savior, was born.

The shepherds left and found the child in a manger and—of course—they were overjoyed and shared this wonderful news with others.

This devotional explores, shares, and celebrates that joyous good news by continuing a centuries-old Christian tradition of setting aside time to prepare for the celebration of Jesus' birth and to anticipate his return. The Advent season of preparation then unfolds in the joy of the twelve days of Christmas and the day of Epiphany.

Good News, Great Joy provides daily devotions for the first Sunday of Advent (December 1, 2024) through Epiphany (January 6, 2025). These devotions explore year C scripture readings (in the Revised Common Lectionary) for the Sundays of Advent and Christmas, as well as for the festival days of Christmas and Epiphany. Each reading is accompanied by an image, a reflection, and a prayer. The writers bring their unique voices and pastoral wisdom to these texts, and offer the voices of other witnesses in the quotations they have chosen for the "To ponder" sections. The devotional also provides household blessings and prayers (see pages 81–93) to enrich your preparations and celebrations during the Advent and Christmas seasons.

Jesus was born for you and for all. May the angel's announcement fill you with great joy and send you out into a world longing for good news!

December 1 / Advent 1

Jeremiah 33:14-15

The days are surely coming, says the LORD, when I will fulfill the promise I made to the house of Israel and the house of Judah. In those days and at that time I will cause a righteous Branch to spring up for David; and he shall execute justice and righteousness in the land.

To ponder

Lo, how a rose e'er blooming from tender stem hath sprung!
Of Jesse's lineage coming as seers of old have sung,
it came, a flow'r so bright, amid the cold of winter,
when half-spent was the night.
—"Lo, How a Rose E'er Blooming," ELW 272

Waiting for the right time

Peace lilies are common houseplants that often come from the florist with large, shiny green leaves and beautiful white flowers. Inevitably, the flowers fade away and the plant, while continuing to look green and healthy, doesn't bloom again. Plant owners often become disappointed—and even get rid of the plants—because they expect the flowers to keep coming. What many people don't know is that plant nurseries use gibberellic acid to force peace lilies to bloom. The blooms are beautiful and help sell plants, but their beauty fades.

In difficult times and in ordinary times, we often wonder what God is up to and when God will bring much-needed newness to the struggles we face. It is tempting to want instant solutions to the problems in our lives and our world. But solutions that bring a quick bloom never last.

God offers something more profound than artificial answers to our real needs: a fulfillment of God's promises that lasts, the strong branch of justice and righteousness, the flower of peace. This cannot be forced by chemicals or manipulation or false promises. This comes through God's careful and patient work in our lives and in the world.

Prayer

O God, grant me patience to wait for all the good things you are doing through Christ Jesus in my life and in the world. Amen.

December 2

Psalm 25:4-5

Show me your ways, O Lord,
and teach me your paths.
Lead me in your truth and teach me,
for you are the God of my salvation;
in you have I trusted all the day long.

To ponder

Complete freedom is not what a trail offers. Quite the opposite; a trail is a tactful reduction of options.—Robert Moor, *On Trails*

Too many choices

Two brothers took a trip to Costa Rica to see the beautiful sites and enjoy the culture. They rented a car to get from place to place. When they arrived in San José, they discovered that their phones did not include a data plan for international travel. That meant no GPS to guide them to beaches, volcanoes, and sloth habitats. They would have a difficult time getting to each destination, and risked getting lost in a place they knew little about. They decided to pay $50 for a week of data service. They needed some GPS guidance or they would get lost on too many turns and roads.

When the psalmist says, "Show me your ways . . . teach me your paths . . . lead me in your truth," they realize there are too many choices to make, too many wrong turns to take. To avoid getting lost they need God's guidance. There will still be choices, but God's teachings about love, justice, and mercy reveal the better options.

When we pray for guidance, we are praying for fewer choices, for fewer wrong turns, for better paths. Having too many choices does not help us or make us free. What we need most is a clear compass to keep us moving in God's ways. As Christians, we find this compass in the life, death, and resurrection of Christ.

Prayer

Jesus, my true north, you are always with me. Guide me in your ways of love, justice, and mercy. Amen.

December 3

1 Thessalonians 3:12-13

May the Lord make you increase and abound in love for one
another and for all, just as we abound in love for you. And
may he so strengthen your hearts in holiness that you may
be blameless before our God and Father at the coming of our
Lord Jesus with all his saints.

To ponder

General opinion's starting to make out that we live in a world
of hatred and greed, but I don't see that. It seems to me that
love is everywhere. Often, it's not particularly dignified or
newsworthy, but it's always there—fathers and sons, mothers

and daughters, husbands and wives, boyfriends, girlfriends, old friends. . . . If you look for it, I've got a sneaky feeling you'll find that love actually is all around.—*Love Actually*

Abound in love

Paul writes and prays that God will make the congregation in Thessalonica increase and abound in love. At first it sounds like the Thessalonians don't have much love for each other. Is that the issue? Certainly there's room for any person or community to become more loving toward others. Or is there something else to this plea and prayer from Paul?

Maybe there is plenty of love in the church at Thessalonica. Otherwise, how could love "increase and abound"? The issue could be that people just don't recognize how much love is in their lives—the love of God, the love of Paul, and the love they have for each other.

A helpful spiritual practice is the act of noticing—paying closer attention to what is around us. How can we become more aware of the ways our lives and our congregations already abound with God's love? How does noticing this cause us to abound in love for others?

Prayer

God of abundance, help us notice the ways you love us and all creation. By your Spirit empower us to abound in love for one another and for all. Amen.

December 4

Luke 21:25, 27-28

[Jesus said,] "There will be signs in the sun, the moon, and the stars, and on the earth distress among nations confused by the roaring of the sea and the waves. . . . Then they will see 'the Son of Man coming in a cloud' with power and great glory. Now when these things begin to take place, stand up and raise your heads, because your redemption is drawing near."

To ponder

It turns out that our visual brains have several distinct systems. One of them is more specialized for the graspable interaction space of the lower visual field and another is specialized for the visual field above the horizon. . . . This area of the brain is strongly activated during religious experiences, meditative activity, dreaming, and probably any kind of artistic or creative activity that encourages us to reach beyond the bounds of nearby time and space into the infinite and eternal. It's no accident . . . that meditative states, trances, mystical or religious experiences are often accompanied by upward deviations of the eyes.—Colin Ellard, "Look Up"

Looking upward

In Luke 21, Jesus talks about cosmic signs and international distress, but instead of telling his followers to hide and cower in fear when these things happen, he tells them to stand up and raise their heads in confidence. Why? Because they are signs that God's redemption is coming near. Jesus encourages his followers to take this stance because God's promised future of goodness is always moving closer.

Different types of prayer use different body positions. One way to pray is with arms outstretched, hands open to the sky, and head raised. Our confidence is in God alone, to whom we pray for a coming kingdom that brings bread and love for all. Pray the Lord's Prayer and the prayer below in a position of open, upward confidence in God.

Prayer

O God, in all times give me confidence in you alone, in Jesus' name. Amen.

Luke 21:29-31

Then [Jesus] told them a parable: "Look at the fig tree and all the trees; as soon as they sprout leaves you can see for yourselves and know that summer is already near. So also, when you see these things taking place, you know that the kingdom of God is near."

To ponder

Serious and solemn words come naturally to the man who feels life escaping him, and the grave opening before him. The depths of his nature are then revealed; the divine within him need no longer hide itself. Oh, do not let us wait to be just or pitiful or demonstrative toward those we love until they or we are struck down by illness or threatened with death! Life is short and we have never too much time for gladdening the hearts of those who are traveling the dark journey with us. Oh, be swift to love, make haste to be kind!—Henri-Frédéric Amiel, *Amiel's Journal*

Seeing and being signs

In today's reading Jesus reminds the disciples that they are on a long journey in life as they await the fulfillment of God's promises. He encourages them to look at the signs that show they are getting closer, or rather that God is close to them already, closer than they can imagine.

What signs help us see that the reigning activity of God is near? Sharing food with people who are hungry? Sheltering refugees who have fled persecution? Spending time with someone who is struggling with life's hardships? Every act of love, mercy, healing, and generosity is a sign that God's reign is closer than we think.

Sometimes we see the signs, and sometimes we live them. In 1898 Henri-Frédéric Amiel wrote that life goes by quickly, so take every opportunity to bring joy and to show kindness to those traveling this earth with us. Celebrate the signs of God's love in our midst—those signs revealed to us and those enacted by us.

Prayer

God of nearness, enliven my imagination so I can see and enact signs of your ever-present love. Amen.

December 6

Luke 21:33
[Jesus said,] "Heaven and earth will pass away, but my words
will not pass away."

To ponder
Swift to its close ebbs out life's little day;
earth's joys grow dim, its glories pass away;
change and decay in all around I see;
O thou who changest not, abide with me.
—"Abide with Me," ELW 629

My word is my bond

Jesus' words in today's reading don't sound very cheery. "Heaven and earth will pass away" is certainly true, but when we remember that "earth" includes all of us, we're reminded that we too will pass away. Everything is temporal and fading, including us small humans, and this does not make for happy thoughts.

Yet, immediately after this less-than-uplifting statement, Jesus says something else: "but my words will not pass away." Ah, there *is* something reliable, lasting, and trustworthy—Jesus' words! But what does this mean—the printed words on a page? Those will disappear with the earth.

There's an old English saying: "My word is my bond." It's the motto for the London Stock Exchange, but it originated centuries ago. It means that what I say is trustworthy because I am trustworthy. If I say it, you can depend on it, because I am dependable.

What is lasting is not simply Jesus' words, but his promise, his love, his enduring presence. Because God in Christ is reliable, trustworthy, and dependable, we can rest in God's words of promise, love, and eternal life. Yes, even we who will pass away can trust in God's resurrection power in Christ, which will carry us through.

Prayer

God of life, remind us of what lasts forever: you, your words, and your love for all in Christ Jesus. Amen.

December 7

Luke 21:34-36

[Jesus said,] "Be on guard so that your hearts are not weighed down with dissipation and drunkenness and the worries of this life, and that day catch you unexpectedly, like a trap. For it will come upon all who live on the face of the whole earth. Be alert at all times."

To ponder

For years now I've been wondering why is there not a news show dedicated entirely to good news. . . . Alright, enough is enough, world. Why not us? Why not now?—John Krasinski, *Some Good News*, episode 1

Some good news

All the bad news in the world and in our lives can weigh us down. A heavy heart can experience anxiety, fear, or depression. All that heaviness can take away our ability to see and enjoy good things that are also happening.

In March of 2020, as the COVID-19 pandemic began to cause quarantines and lockdowns, actor John Krasinski started a YouTube channel from his home, called *Some Good News*. He did it to help people realize that there was some good news even in this incredibly difficult time. In each YouTube episode, people shared good news stories and lifted each other's spirits.

In today's text Jesus says, "Be alert at all times." That doesn't just mean staying awake. It means being attentive to the good God is doing even when it feels like the world is falling apart. Being aware of and telling others about the good news of God lifts our spirits and keeps us hopeful and alert as we await all the good things God has promised for us in Christ.

Prayer

God of all good things, keep us alert to the good things you are doing in the world. Lift our heavy hearts so we can lift others with the good news of Jesus. Amen.

December 8 / Advent 2

Philippians 1:3-6

I thank my God every time I remember you, constantly praying with joy in every one of my prayers for all of you, because of your sharing in the gospel from the first day until now. I am confident of this, that the one who began a good work among you will bring it to completion by the day of Jesus Christ.

To ponder

You are a human being. You are always arriving.—Kaitlin B. Curtice, *Living Resistance*

God at work

In this pastoral letter to the people of Philippi, the apostle Paul and Timothy begin by offering gratitude for this community. It is a fitting entry into this second week of Advent to hear gratitude for our role in community. God made us for community, to be in loving relationship with each other.

The reality of life is that our communities are not always loving or supportive. They tend to be messy, complicated, and full of unfulfilled expectations. Sometimes we feel like the object of those unfulfilled expectations, and sometimes we feel like the cause of the messiness!

In this season of Advent, we are waiting—waiting for Christmas, waiting for Christ to return, waiting for God's vision of the world to be made known here on earth. And all the while we also know that we, as a community and as individuals, are called by our baptismal promises not just to sit and wait, but to actively work for peace and justice in all the earth. This call can be overwhelming, so I encourage you to take time to dwell in the waiting. The work is not finished, and that is okay. God is still at work in you and in your community.

Prayer

God, for whom we wait, you shape us together for your good purpose. Help us offer compassion and patience to one another and ourselves, as we become who you call us to be. Amen.

December 9

Philippians 1:9-11

This is my prayer, that your love may overflow more and more with knowledge and full insight to help you to determine what is best, so that in the day of Christ you may be pure and blameless, having produced the harvest of righteousness that comes through Jesus Christ for the glory and praise of God.

To ponder

[One] of the things that Maya taught me to understand, . . . she would say, "Those people who are talking about you out there cannot hold a candle to the light God already has shining on your face. Can you see the light? Can you feel the light?" —Oprah Winfrey on Maya Angelou, in "Chief to Chief"

Praying with and for others

I love to pray with and for children and youth, as the apostle Paul and Timothy did for the Philippians and as Maya did for Oprah. Our young people can discern the authenticity of my heart in my prayer. They know in their beings the difference between a manipulative prayer and one of sincere care. And when they experience sincere prayers said for them, over them, and with them, they learn to pray for each other, for the world, and even for me.

Being prayed over by children is a powerful experience, and I commend it to you as a necessary spiritual practice in your life. Often, over the course of my ministry with children and youth, I have had to share with them the news of difficult times in my life: the death of a loved one, a scary medical diagnosis, the closing of my time with them, and so on. These beautiful young people have responded by offering to pray for me. Their prayers revealed the hurt I was feeling and the hope I needed. And together we would wait for God in that hope.

Prayer

God of love, give us vulnerable hearts to share our burdens and joys with our community, that in praying for one another, we would not despair, but rather learn to wait in hope for your promised return. Amen.

December 10

Luke 1:68-71

[Zechariah said:]
"Blessed be the Lord God of Israel,
for he has looked favorably on his people and redeemed them.
He has raised up a mighty savior for us
in the house of his servant David,
as he spoke through the mouth of his holy prophets from of old,
that we would be saved from our enemies."

To ponder

To pay attention, this is our endless and proper work.—Mary Oliver, "Yes! No!"

God pays us a visit

When our kids were young and I was a new pastor, my mother lived an hour away. When she paid a visit, she never gave any forewarning. She often called me at church around noon: "I'm in town. Where's lunch?" Once, when I had a yard project in mind, she called early on a Saturday morning: "Your uncle and I will show up shortly. Let's do your project." This often irritated me, but if I could make time, her visits were very enjoyable—and productive. The God we know in Christ shows up in our lives in similar ways: suddenly, unexpectedly, testing our openness to change. But as we embrace these visits, they change us for good.

Zechariah's words kick off a longer prophecy (Luke 1:68-79). He praises God who has "looked favorably" on God's people. The Greek verb used here is often translated as "visited." In biblical writings, God's visits are often favorable and bring salvation. The idea is this: God cannot save from a distance. In Christ, God draws near—pays us a visit—to save us.

Imagine Christ paying you a visit. How might God be drawing near this season—to assist you, help you hold it together, be there for you, or save you? Zechariah praised the One who "has visited and redeemed" us. In Christ, this God continues to visit us today.

Prayer

O God, help us embrace the holy and unexpected ways you visit us this season, through Christ our Lord. Amen.

December 11

Luke 1:76-78

[Zechariah continued:]
"And you, child, will be called the prophet of the Most High;
for you will go before the Lord to prepare his ways,
to give knowledge of salvation to his people
by the forgiveness of their sins.
By the tender mercy of our God,
the dawn from on high will break upon us."

To ponder

Faith is the bird that feels the light and sings when the dawn is
still dark.—Rabindranath Tagore, *Fireflies*

Singing before dawn

When our kids were young, I often took them camping. We camped with sleeping bags in a tent. While my kids slept, I spent time thinking. And in the absence of a clock, I could easily tell when dawn approached: by the birds. A full hour before dawn, the fulsome noise of birdsong filled the dark in impressive ways. Like clockwork, the birds knew precisely when dawn was coming—and they welcomed it with song.

John the Baptizer was called to prepare the way for Jesus. Like a songbird, John announced salvation by the forgiveness of sin and the tender mercy of God. It wasn't a glamorous job. But the foretold arrival was worth singing about.

Zechariah's prophecy about John has a beautiful metaphor: "The dawn from on high will break upon us." Building upon Old Testament precedents, this language marks the arrival of salvation in John's time, through the person of Jesus. Like the arrival of dawn, Christ ushers in a salvation that changes everything, filling the world with healing and life.

Like John, we are called to sing before the arrival of dawn—only, in our case that dawn is the ultimate arrival of salvation through Jesus' return. Meanwhile, we celebrate his arrivals at Bethlehem and in our hearts today.

Prayer

O Dawn from on High, O Christ who gives life to our weary souls, give us faith to see your salvation during our darkest hours—and to sing loudly. Amen.

December 12

Malachi 3:1

See, I am sending my messenger to prepare the way before me, and the Lord whom you seek will suddenly come to his temple. The messenger of the covenant in whom you delight—indeed, he is coming, says the LORD of hosts.

To ponder

Anticipation and hope are born twins.—Jean-Jacque Rousseau

Preparation and anticipation

In our family, I'm the vacation planner. I have this role because no one else wants it. But I like it. It helps me anticipate experiences to come. My daughter is similar. She likes to know how long it is until our vacation, how long we will travel, and what we will do. It gives us something to look forward to during the school year's toughest slogs. When we return from a trip, we get a bit depressed. The reason: anticipation is part of the experience.

Advent is a season of preparation and anticipation of Jesus' arrival. The book of Malachi describes "my messenger" (*mala-chi*, in Hebrew) who will prepare the way. After this, the Lord "will suddenly come." The passage's immediacy invites us to be prepared, since we don't know the time of the Lord's arrival.

Preparation and anticipation help us get ready for arrivals. Without preparing our homes, we cannot welcome guests well. Without preparing ourselves, we cannot fully embrace God's gifts. Without preparing our hearts, we cannot faithfully welcome Christ in.

Preparation and anticipation move us to hope. Psychologists suggest that anticipating good things helps our moods and stress levels. For Christians, anticipating Christ's arrival is part of our calling. We are called to prepare ourselves for Christ and to live in hope of his salvation.

Prayer

O holy child of Bethlehem, descend to us, we pray;
cast out our sin, and enter in, be born in us today.
We hear the Christmas angels the great glad tidings tell;
oh, come to us, abide with us, our Lord Immanuel!
—"O Little Town of Bethlehem," ELW 279

December 13

Luke 3:1-2

In the fifteenth year of the reign of Emperor Tiberius, when Pontius Pilate was governor of Judea, and Herod was ruler of Galilee, and his brother Philip ruler of the region of Ituraea and Trachonitis, and Lysanias ruler of Abilene, during the high priesthood of Annas and Caiaphas, the word of God came to John son of Zechariah in the wilderness.

To ponder

To live in the present, we must believe deeply that what is most important is the here and now. We are constantly distracted by things that have happened in the past or that might happen in the future. . . . If we could just be, for a few minutes each day, fully where we are, we would indeed discover that we are not alone and that the One who is with us wants only one thing: to give us love.—Henri J. M. Nouwen, *Here and Now*

The here and now

More than any other gospel writer, Luke grounds his story in history. In telling us about John the Baptizer, Luke begins with the historical realities of his day. Luke tells us who was emperor (Tiberius), who governed Judea (Pontius Pilate), who ruled Galilee (Herod), who ruled surrounding areas (Philip and Lysanias), and who were high priests (Annas and Caiaphas). Luke packs these verses with more historical information than we ever wanted to know.

However seemingly mundane, these details imply something significant: God is at work in real-life times and places. God doesn't act in the abstract, but in the real world. God is present and active in the here and now, right where we are, closer at hand than we realize. This idea isn't rocket science. But we tend to forget it. God is right here, right now. God is at work today.

Take a few minutes to ponder this. Pray the prayer below in silence. Repeat and let it sink in. Embrace the nearness of God with you today.

Prayer

God, you are here with me. Christ, you are here with me. Holy Spirit, you are here with me. Amen.

December 14

Luke 3:3-4

[John] went into all the region around the Jordan, proclaiming a baptism of repentance for the forgiveness of sins, as it is written in the book of the words of the prophet Isaiah,
"The voice of one crying out in the wilderness:
'Prepare the way of the Lord, make his paths straight.'"

To ponder

Razing things to the ground is easy. Trying to fix what's broken is hard. Hope is hard.— Loki, in "Heart of the TVA" (Disney+, 2023)

Hope is hard

Hope is hard. It takes time and energy. It flies in the face of a world that nurtures cynicism, criticism, and pessimism. Most days it's easier to resign ourselves to pessimism. That way we will never be disappointed. But God has better things for us.

John the Baptizer is a man of undeterred hope. Whether or not he looks like a poster boy for hopefulness, he lives it: he gathers crowds in the wilderness, calling them to prepare for a savior he has not met, trusting that his prophetic vocation is not in vain. Dressed in camel's hair and eating locusts and honey, he probably seems nuts to some people. But he keeps on keeping on, trusting that God will prove faithful.

Hope is hard. But it is simply faith turned toward the future. Christian hope is not based in naïve optimism or superficial assessments. It's grounded in the steadfast love of God made known in Christ, and it trusts that because nothing can separate us from God's love in Christ Jesus, all shall be well. Christian hope is grounded in the surest reality that exists: God.

Hope is hard. But the God of the resurrected Christ calls us to be a people of hope, for the sake of a weary, cynical world. Hope is hard—and desperately needed today.

Prayer

O God of steadfast hope, ground us in the love of Christ, and empower us by your Holy Spirit, that we may embody faith, hope, and love in this weary world. Amen.

December 15 / Advent 3

Luke 3:10-11

The crowds [that came to be baptized by John] asked him, "What then should we do?" In reply he said to them, "Whoever has two coats must share with anyone who has none; and whoever has food must do likewise."

To ponder

Have you ever experienced the joy of giving? I do not want you to give to me out of your abundance. . . . I want you to give of yourself. The love you put into the giving is the most important thing.—Mother Teresa, *No Greater Love*

Sacrificial love

The church I served had a relationship with a village in Honduras. We traveled there each year. Once we visited a woman's home. She was a single parent of many children. Her home was tiny and extremely humble by our standards. She owned very little. But she welcomed us. She gave us each a batch of almonds—produce from her work. There were fifteen of us. It was profoundly generous, and we felt awkward receiving. But she would not let us refuse. If measured in personal sacrifice, her gift was enormous.

John calls people to share with those in need as a sign of repentance. Many did not have two coats or abundant food, making his words challenging. Yet, he didn't say, "Spare a few bucks" or "Share if you're comfortable." He asked people to give of themselves. That's sacrificial giving.

God calls us to sacrificial giving because it reflects how God loves us. Christ is the ultimate act of sacrificial love. As we have received, we are called to give. This Advent, how might you try forms of sacrificial love? Generosity is not measured simply in dollars, but also in time, care, and concern. As Mother Teresa suggests, there is joy in giving. And the most important thing is the love we invest.

Prayer

God, help us live out sacrificial generosity, walking in Jesus' footsteps, that the joy and love of Christ may be fully known. Amen.

Luke 3:15-16

As the people were filled with expectation, and all were questioning in their hearts concerning John, whether he might be the Messiah, John answered all of them by saying, "I baptize you with water; but one who is more powerful than I is coming; I am not worthy to untie the thong of his sandals. He will baptize you with the Holy Spirit and fire."

To ponder

Midsummer night, and bonfires on the hill
Burn for the man who makes way for the Light:
'He must increase and I diminish still,
Until his sun illuminates my night.'
So John the Baptist pioneers our path,

Unfolds the essence of the life of prayer,
Unlatches the last doorway into faith,
And makes one inner space an everywhere.
—Malcolm Guite, "St. John the Baptist"

Pointing people to Jesus

We know John the Baptizer from the gospels. Here he's a messenger who prepares the way for Jesus. Consistent with this calling, John points people to Jesus as one more worthy of attention.

Many of us don't realize just how famous John was. The first-century Jewish historian Josephus portrays John as a powerful preacher with a significant following—so big that it made Herod the Great nervous. In a time long before social media, John was an influencer. Influential as he was, John directed people to Jesus. John didn't do it as a humble brag or for unhealthy reasons. He did it because it was his God-given calling.

You and I are similarly called to point people to Jesus. We are called to name how he has changed our lives for the better. We do this not to devalue ourselves or to underappreciate our work. We do it to identify who has saved our souls and transformed our futures.

Prayer

O Christ, as John directed focus toward you, help us set our sights upon you, that we may welcome you most fully in our midst and in our hearts. Amen.

December 17

Zephaniah 3:14-15

Sing aloud, O daughter Zion;
shout, O Israel!
Rejoice and exult with all your heart,
O daughter Jerusalem!
The Lord has taken away the judgments against you,
he has turned away your enemies.
The king of Israel, the Lord, is in your midst;
you shall fear disaster no more.

To ponder

Since Christ is Lord of heaven and earth,
how can I keep from singing?
—"My Life Flows On in Endless Song," ELW 763

If you have Christ, you have everything

During my first year of seminary, one morning I was especially discouraged. My studies raised more questions than answers. My hospital chaplaincy work was challenging. My prayer life was stale. So I sat in silence. After some time, I came to a sudden realization of Christ's presence with me. I can't say just how. But it was very real. Suddenly all the challenges and questions I faced looked smaller—not the crushing issues I had thought they were. Christ was with me. What need I fear?

Zephaniah announces God's promise to restore Jerusalem and return its exiles home. The prophet invites hearers to "sing aloud" and "rejoice . . . with all your heart," not just because of the changes in fortune but because "the Lord is in your midst." In response, "you shall fear disaster no more."

Life is full of challenges, pain, and sorrow. Zephaniah reminds us that with the Lord in our midst, we need not fear the worst. As Christians, we may say it this way: If you have Christ, you have everything. As Martin Luther preached on Christmas Day in 1530: "[Christ] is the Savior. And if this is true—and it is the truth—then let everything else go."

Life is full of challenges and difficulties. But if Christ is Savior and Lord—and he is—we may joyfully let our worst worries go.

Prayer

O Christ, help us trust you with our lives, place our burdens into your hands, and sing your praise. Amen.

December 18

Zephaniah 3:20

At that time I will bring you home,
at the time when I gather you;
for I will make you renowned and praised
among all the peoples of the earth,
when I restore your fortunes
before your eyes, says the LORD.

To ponder

God of our weary years, God of our silent tears,
thou who hast brought us thus far on the way;
thou who hast by thy might led us into the light,
keep us forever in the path, we pray.
—"Lift Every Voice and Sing," ELW 841

Sure and certain hope

Henri Nouwen tells a story about a man who was imprisoned. Without a clear timeline for his release, he began to despair. Nothing motivated him to press on. Then one day a letter came from a friend. It said, essentially, "We are waiting for you, and we look forward to seeing you again." It changed everything. The man suddenly went from despair to hope, because he knew that someone was waiting for him beyond this season. He could live in hope, knowing that a better future was on the horizon.

The promise of a better future can move us from despair to hope as well. A great many things in our world weigh us down with anxiety, fear, uncertainty, and hopelessness. Some days it's tough just to get out of bed and keep going. But the God who, through Zephaniah and others, promised restoration to exiles—the God we know in Jesus Christ—promises resurrection on the other side of death. This God entered our hopeless world as a babe in Bethlehem to set us free from sin, death, and despair. This God promises us a future far superior to the sufferings of this present time.

Through Christ, God promises us a homecoming just on the horizon. This Christmas season, we celebrate that hope as our guiding star through nights of despair.

Prayer

O God of life beyond death, help us to live in sure and certain hope that we have a glorious future in you. Amen.

December 19

Philippians 4:4-7

Rejoice in the Lord always; again I will say, Rejoice. Let your gentleness be known to everyone. The Lord is near. Do not worry about anything, but in everything by prayer and supplication with thanksgiving let your requests be made known to God. And the peace of God, which surpasses all understanding, will guard your hearts and your minds in Christ Jesus.

To ponder

Don't ask what the world needs. Ask what makes you come alive and go out and do it, because what the world needs is people who have come alive.—Howard Thurman, in *Violence Unveiled*

What makes you come alive?

The season of Advent and Paul's letter to the Philippians are filled with calls for joy and rejoicing that can feel counter to worldly calls for work, labor, and consumption. While the world would have us believe that the source of our joy is found in achievements, accomplishments, and shiny purchases, the truth is that none of those things can guarantee our happiness—and more likely will only pull us further from true joy.

The joy to which we are invited this season may not look like worldly happiness, because it's less a feeling and more a state of being, a way of living. As we give thanks to and put our trust in God, we find a peace that becomes our joy. We bring God's vision for the world closer by loving and serving our neighbor, and knowing this removes some of the worry and distress in our lives.

As you wait this Advent season, know that God wants you to experience deep joy. Seek out God's joy for you. Trust that what makes you come alive is how God is calling you to love and serve your neighbors in the world.

Prayer

Generous God, stir our hearts to see clearly what is life-giving and love-affirming in our lives. Help us see these things as your gifts of joy. Teach us to rejoice in you always. Amen.

December 20

Isaiah 12:2

Surely God is my salvation;
I will trust, and will not be afraid,
for the Lord God is my strength and my might;
he has become my salvation.

To ponder

How come nobody told me an aria, a piece of stained glass,
a painting, a sunset can be God too?—Sandra Cisneros, *A
House of My Own*

What are we waiting for?

For most of my adult life I have lived near or below the pov-
erty line, so when our family's financial circumstances changed,

it was a shock to my system. For so long we had put off any purchase that wasn't deemed a necessity. Then suddenly we were able to splurge on fun things with little concern or worry. We paid off the credit cards, upgraded our phones, joined a gym, bought a house, and purchased new (to us) cars. In the eyes of the world, we were living the dream. We had achieved a life for which we had been waiting—but it didn't bring peace of mind or heart. It didn't free us from systems of oppression, and it still left us wondering who we could trust, feeling fearful of new things and helpless when our children's hearts were hurting.

What are we waiting for during this Advent season? The trap of capitalism says we are waiting for Christmas gifts, as if making the right purchases will make our holiday bright. But all the fancy presents we can buy will not save our Christmas. We are not likely to find God, our strength and might and salvation, there. I invite you to remember that the One for whom we wait shows up every day in beautiful, priceless ways. The One for whom we wait is creating beauty before your very eyes, and wants you to see it right now.

Prayer

God who waits, thank you for giving us the spiritual practice of patience and waiting. Grant us trusting hearts to see you every day, in every person we meet. Amen.

December 21

Isaiah 12:4-6

Give thanks to the LORD, call on his name;
make known his deeds among the nations;
proclaim that his name is exalted.
Sing praises to the LORD, for he has done gloriously;
let this be known in all the earth.
Shout aloud and sing for joy, O royal Zion,
for great in your midst is the Holy One of Israel.

To ponder

We are waiting for Jesus; Jesus brings peace. . . .
Sun of justice, . . . walk beside us;

stir our hearts and gently guide us.
We are waiting for Jesus; Jesus brings peace.
—"We Are Waiting for Jesus," ACS 905

Even on this longest night

The Advent season has moved us deeper and deeper into the darkness of this, the longest night of the year. With Advent candles and Christmas lights, we honor this darkness as a place from which peace and joy will come. During this long night, we feel the anguish of our hurting world, witness the empty chairs of loved ones gone too soon, and honor our grief. This longest night is an opportunity to see the whole season of Advent as leading to this moment when lament and sorrow are welcome guests.

The blessing of this night is that we have reached the depth of the darkness, and yet we can see the stars. We know the sun is coming back. Even on this night, we can rejoice as we wait. We can give thanks for all who walk beside us in times of sorrow and times of joy, and for the ones who watch and wait with us in the shadows. We can sing praise to the Holy One in our midst. In the light of the stars, we can rejoice that Christ is coming, bringing sunshine, justice, peace, and love.

Prayer

God of starlight, during this longest night, be with all who hurt. Be with all who watch and wait. Bring your peace to a world that longs for good news. Amen.

December 22 / Advent 4

Luke 1:39-42

In those days Mary set out and went with haste to a Judean town in the hill country, where she entered the house of Zechariah and greeted Elizabeth. When Elizabeth heard Mary's greeting, the child leaped in her womb. And Elizabeth was filled with the Holy Spirit and exclaimed with a loud cry, "Blessed are you among women, and blessed is the fruit of your womb."

To ponder

Your heart's desire will fill your mouth, your actions, and your labor. You will know what you love by what you say, where you

go, and what you do. Your heart's desire is easily revealed.—
Meister Eckhart, *Meditations on the Path of the Wayless Way*

Surprise!

My husband and in-laws surprised me recently with a birthday
party. My birthday was a few days away, so it was not even on
my radar. I was distracted, texting on my phone as I walked
into the living room. As a result, they had to surprise me twice!
When I finally grasped that the surprise was for me, I was
overwhelmed with gratitude. I laughed and danced around
the room, gave hugs, and beamed the rest of the evening. It
revealed how much celebrating with others means to me.

Elizabeth is surprised too and cries out with a loud voice,
making a great clamor. In the Greek New Testament, it's
almost as if the author can't express how excited Elizabeth is
as she bubbles over with joy and delight. Somehow, after hearing Mary's greeting, Elizabeth knows something wonderful is
afoot for her and for all people. The Spirit, active within her,
reveals what is important to her: awaiting and celebrating the
coming Messiah. She might be surprised at how it happens,
but her delight reveals the depth of her longing and gratitude.

What might be revealed as God surprises you in this time
of Advent waiting?

Prayer

Mysterious God, may my heart long for you. Surprise and
delight me as you show up. Amen.

December 23

Luke 2:1-4

In those days a decree went out from Emperor Augustus that all the world should be registered. This was the first registration and was taken while Quirinius was governor of Syria. All went to their own towns to be registered. Joseph also went from the town of Nazareth in Galilee to Judea, to the city of David called Bethlehem, because he was descended from the house and family of David.

To ponder

We are all on this journey of life together, each given certain gifts to make this world a better place and to help make one another's burdens a little lighter along the way.—Mike Ramsdell, *A Train to Potevka*

Journeying

Nativity displays don't often capture the questions, turmoil, heartbreak, and tragedy that were part of the story. Today's photo shows a family, excitedly gathered around a nativity, learning and growing in faith. The holy family, portrayed in crèches like this one, also learned and grew through their experiences, including a journey they were forced to make because of the emperor's decree—a journey that helped shape their story.

What difficult, even unwanted, journeys have shaped your story or caused you to learn and grow? The polished lives we portray, perceive, and consume often conceal what has impacted us and those who've helped along the way. We sanitize our stories, uncertain of whether it's safe to be vulnerable, perhaps thinking everyone else has things figured out while we struggle to keep it together. But we are all journeying, learning to truly love God, ourselves, and our neighbor. We get to accompany each other as we travel through life, sharing compassion, comfort, patience, and peace. The mystery of the incarnation shows that God is willing to voyage as a human and is pleased to journey with us. We never travel alone.

Prayer

Jesus, journey with us into the territory of authentic, loving relationship and community. Amen.

December 24 / Christmas Eve

Luke 2:5-7

[Joseph] went to be registered with Mary, to whom he was engaged and who was expecting a child. While they were [in Bethlehem], the time came for her to deliver her child. And she gave birth to her firstborn son and wrapped him in bands of cloth, and laid him in a manger, because there was no place for them in the inn.

To ponder

Love has come and never will leave us!
—"Love Has Come," ELW 292

Love holds us

God is born—naked, crying, afraid, hungry—and completely dependent on nervous, overwhelmed, exhausted, uncertain people for nurturing and protection. The creator of all becomes the one in need of tending, feeding, protection, teaching, and raising. God wants so much to hold us and draw us close that God becomes a newborn so we will cradle the holy tenderly in our arms.

Holding an infant can be a scary experience: "Am I doing this right? What if he's not comfortable? What if she cries? How will I know what to do for this baby?" Perhaps the same could be said of our relationship to God, often full of worry and doubt, uncertainty, or even discomfort. But when an infant looks at you, full of hopeful trust, love desires to do everything possible to care for that little one. The incarnation of Jesus is love rushing into our lives, propelled by God's desire to do everything possible to care for us. Paradoxically, while beholding the fragility and vulnerability of the infant Jesus, we realize that God is always holding us.

It's a bewildering grace that in this babe, we learn what love looks like. How might God be inviting you to gently hold and tend the holy in your life this Christmas season?

Prayer

Thank you, God, for your vulnerable love that relies on everyday people. Amen.

December 25 / Christmas

Luke 2:8-12

In that region there were shepherds living in the fields, keeping watch over their flock by night. Then an angel of the Lord stood before them, and the glory of the Lord shone around them, and they were terrified. But the angel said to them, "Do not be afraid; for see—I am bringing you good news of great joy for all the people: to you is born this day in the city of David a Savior, who is the Messiah, the Lord. This will be a sign for you: you will find a child wrapped in bands of cloth and lying in a manger."

To ponder

Evening and morning, sunset and dawning. . . .
Times without number, awake or in slumber,
your eye observes us, from danger preserves us,
causing your mercy upon us to shine.
—"Evening and Morning," ELW 761

Keeping watch

The shepherds were terrified when an angel appeared. Has
good news ever felt terrifying to you? New beginnings often
seem fragile—or even scary—because the unknown contains
both opportunity and challenge. As a child, did you ever flop
into freshly fallen snow to make a snow angel? It was a little
frightening, falling backward, but once on the ground, you
were held by the snow as you played with abandon.

The shepherds kept watch over their flock by night. It's
because God is a trustworthy shepherd, watchfully tending
us and seeing precisely what we need to flourish, that Jesus is
born. The good news of great joy is that God is always with
us, and God never slumbers or sleeps (see Psalm 121). We're
invited to trust God's care, free to play and find rest from our
striving because it never was and never is all on us. How might
you celebrate and delight in the angel's good news today?

Prayer

Steadfast God, help us let go of the need to control, entrusting
ourselves and our neighbors to your keeping. Amen.

December 26

Luke 2:13-15

And suddenly there was with the angel a multitude of the heavenly host, praising God and saying, "Glory to God in the highest heaven, and on earth peace among those whom he favors!" When the angels had left them and gone into heaven, the shepherds said to one another, "Let us go now to Bethlehem and see this thing that has taken place, which the Lord has made known to us."

To ponder

[God helps] the poor, despised, afflicted, miserable, forsaken. ... The heart overflows with gladness and goes leaping and dancing for the great pleasure it has found in God. And there the Holy Spirit is present and has taught us in a moment such exceeding great knowledge and gladness.—Martin Luther, "The Magnificat"

Broadway calling

Have you ever watched a Broadway show or movie musical and thought, *Who bursts into fully choreographed, harmonized musical numbers in real life?* It might seem utterly ridiculous, but what if there was something so overwhelmingly, cosmically joyous that it made even the angels sing together?

Messengers of God huddled together (a choir on heavenly risers!), singing off the same sheet music—notes written and breathed by the Holy Spirit flowing through them. What would it take for us, as earthly messengers of God, to be moved to songs of praise and the sharing of good news of great joy with those around us? Why are we usually hesitant to add our voices to the choir? I hesitate because I worry about what others might think—or what I imagine others might be thinking.

The angel choir forms in a silent night—in a rich silence that gives shepherds and angels, you and me, ears to hear from God. It's in listening to and trusting God's voice, not the worried-about whispers, that we find we're free to sing and rejoice, to go and tell good news. Maybe even with jazz hands!

Prayer

Holy Spirit, move through us to live, breathe, sing, and dance the joy of your unending love! Amen.

Luke 2:16-20

So [the shepherds] went with haste and found Mary and Joseph, and the child lying in the manger. When they saw this, they made known what had been told them about this child; and all who heard it were amazed at what the shepherds told them.

To ponder

When it's over, I want to say: all my life
I was a bride married to amazement.
I was the bridegroom, taking the world into my arms.
—Mary Oliver, "Poem 102: When Death Comes"

Wonder-full

The big day of Christmas has come and gone; there are now only leftovers and trash bags full of wrapping paper and packaging. Sometimes I crave the dopamine hit of new, fun things, but then the excitement wears off quickly and I long for something newer, bigger, better, shinier. The life of faith can be like that—after the initial excitement, our zeal wears off, or a profound experience of God fades into the background.

What if the wonder and amazement at finding the baby in the manger could last well beyond Christmas Day? I'm not sure the baby Jesus *looked* miraculous, but people were amazed because the shepherds—probably amazed themselves—talked about who the child was and what his birth meant for the world. Finding amazement in something so seemingly ordinary meant seeing beyond appearances and having faith in a message shared from person to person. Shared joy, wonder, excitement, and even confusion created community.

Through the lens of faith and amazement, how might you observe and perceive Jesus' presence in your midst, right here, right now—and in everyday life? How might sharing these experiences ripple outward, encouraging others to find amazement in the ordinary?

Prayer

Unfathomable God, teach me to live in wonder—in childlike amazement at who you are. Amen.

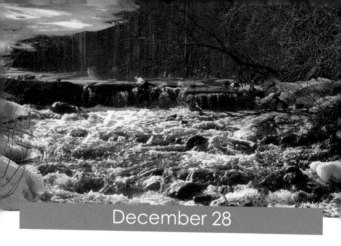

December 28

Titus 3:4-7

When the goodness and loving kindness of God our Savior
appeared, he saved us, not because of any works of righteousness that we had done, but according to his mercy, through the
water of rebirth and renewal by the Holy Spirit. This Spirit
he poured out on us richly through Jesus Christ our Savior, so
that, having been justified by his grace, we might become heirs
according to the hope of eternal life.

To ponder

When you experience mercy, you learn things that are hard to
learn otherwise. You see things you can't otherwise see; you
hear things you can't otherwise hear. You begin to recognize

the humanity that resides in each of us.—Bryan Stevenson, *Just Mercy*

Thin ice

When stressed, in need of solace or inspiration, my feet carry me into the woods and down to the Potomac River. I don't quite understand it, but somehow, observing the forest and the wildlife or watching the river roll by restores my soul and helps me open up to God. One December day in 2022, my husband and I walked to the river, where ice draped everything after heavy rains had quickly frozen over the landscape. Reaching the riverbank, we stood watching ice chunks float down the swiftly moving river.

Today's words from Titus are a river of grace flowing through the wilderness of our lives. The Holy Spirit is full of this wild grace that can break up icy hearts. Looking at a frozen stream or river, sometimes you can spy water moving underneath what seems to be an impenetrable surface. When situations seem frozen solid, unmoving, or at best, moving at a glacial pace, it's difficult to see the current of God's Spirit of mercy. But God's love and grace can flow in the most unexpected places, fitting in the tiniest of cracks until the ice of indifference, anger, and hurt cracks or thaws. Thank you, God!

Prayer

Wild Spirit, warm my heart, May your mercy and grace flow freely in and through me. Amen.

December 29 / Christmas 1

Luke 2:41-44

Now every year [Mary and Joseph] went to Jerusalem for the festival of the Passover. And when [Jesus] was twelve years old, they went up as usual for the festival. When the festival was ended and they started to return, the boy Jesus stayed behind in Jerusalem, but his parents did not know it. Assuming that he was in the group of travelers, they went a day's journey. Then they started to look for him among their relatives and friends.

To ponder

Faith is not the clinging to a shrine but an endless pilgrimage of the heart.—Abraham Joshua Heschel, *Man Is Not Alone*

Pilgrimage

Every year the family joined their relatives and friends to walk three days from Nazareth to Jerusalem for the six days of the festival of Passover, and then spent a few more days returning home. This pilgrimage usually lasted about twelve days, but this year would be different for Mary and Joseph. Little did they know that their plans would go awry as they searched the city for their son.

Many people's plans for the holidays include spending time with friends and family, preparing food and gifts, or worshiping at a church service. As the holy days approach, careful plans change in unexpected and perhaps unwanted ways. Our friends made plans to travel this year, so we can't get together. Children and grandchildren announce they want gift cards for Christmas, not realizing we purchased and wrapped their gifts weeks ago. Family members are not interested in attending Christmas Eve worship with us.

As we look toward a new year, it may be time to reconsider our pilgrimages and our expectations of others. How might we strive to find the holy in each day? How might our celebrations show patience and kindness toward those we love, and care and concern for those in need?

Prayer

God, strengthen my faith and help me create daily pilgrimages of joy. Amen.

December 30

Luke 2:46-49

After three days [Mary and Joseph] found [Jesus] in the temple, sitting among the teachers, listening to them and asking them questions. And all who heard him were amazed at his understanding and his answers. When his parents saw him they were astonished; and his mother said to him, "Child, why have you treated us like this? Look, your father and I have been searching for you in great anxiety." He said to them, "Why were you searching for me? Did you not know that I must be in my Father's house?"

To ponder

I wonder as I wander, out under the sky,
how Jesus the Savior did come for to die

for poor ordinary people like you and like I;
I wonder as I wander, out under the sky.

When Mary birthed Jesus, 'twas in a cow's stall
with wise men and farmers and shepherds and all.
But high from God's heaven a star's light did fall,
and the promise of ages it did then recall.
—John Jacob Niles, "I Wonder as I Wander"

Wonder

The teachers in the temple were amazed at the insight of a twelve-year-old boy. Perhaps Jesus was lost in wonderment too at all he was learning and sharing with these teachers. Mary and Joseph, meanwhile, were upset and "astonished" to find Jesus in the temple after searching for him for three days.

This story may seem out of place at this point in the Christmas season. The wonder of Christmas pageants and celebrations is behind us, and we're starting to get back to the usual grind. Yet this account encourages us to stop and take notice. At twelve years old, Jesus amazes everyone in the temple with his questions and answers! This should give us pause too, and invite us to wonder: How can this be? Who does Jesus think he is? Who do *we* think he is?

Prayer

Gracious God, in our wondering and wandering, thank you for your wondrous love. Amen.

December 31

Luke 2:51-52

Then [Jesus] went down with [Mary and Joseph] and came to Nazareth, and was obedient to them. His mother treasured all these things in her heart.

And Jesus increased in wisdom and in years, and in divine and human favor.

To ponder

We must grow up in every way into him who is the head, into Christ, from whom the whole body, joined and knit together by every ligament with which it is equipped, as each part is working properly, promotes the body's growth in building itself up in love.—Ephesians 4:15-16

Growth

"Jesus increased in wisdom and in years, and in divine and human favor." Many years of Jesus' life are summed up in that sentence! Jesus had time to learn and grow during these years before his ministry of preaching, teaching, and healing began.

Learning and growing are gifts from God. We respond to these gifts by being curious about the world around us, taking in and processing new knowledge, and learning from experience. In today's world we have endless opportunities to broaden our knowledge by finding out about our own and other countries, learning a new language, keeping up with the latest breakthroughs in science and medicine, and so on. When we learn about other cultures and peoples, our lives are enriched with new ideas, greater understanding, and broader horizons.

We have endless opportunities to learn and grow in faith too, by praying, reading and studying the Bible, worshiping with other believers, serving people in need, and working for justice and peace in the world. The Spirit uses all these things and more to nurture us and help us "grow up" in Christ.

Prayer

God, help us grow in faith, love, and compassion for the world and all your people. Amen.

January 1

Colossians 3:12-14

As God's chosen ones, holy and beloved, clothe yourselves with compassion, kindness, humility, meekness, and patience. Bear with one another and, if anyone has a complaint against another, forgive each other; just as the Lord has forgiven you, so you also must forgive. Above all, clothe yourselves with love, which binds everything together in perfect harmony.

To ponder

You will know you have forgiven someone when you are able to pray God's best intentions in their life.—Joretta L. Marshall, *How Can I Forgive?*

Living in community

As a new year begins, we hear about repentance and forgiveness, two processes that are crucial to our life together. We carefully undertake both with prayers for God's help and guidance. Repentance means "turning away" from sin. It's a process of admitting what we have done, apologizing to those we have wronged, looking for and acting on ways to make things right, and resolving to not repeat what we did.

Forgiveness means letting go of the anger or resentment that results from another person or group hurting us in some way. It doesn't give anyone permission to repeatedly harm us. Forgiveness often comes more easily when a person sincerely apologizes for the hurt they have caused, and works at making things right again. What do we do when those who hurt us don't even recognize the pain they caused, or they refuse to apologize? And what do we do when circumstances won't allow us to express our forgiveness to the other person or group? A trusted friend, pastor, or other professional can be of help in working through questions like these.

God has forgiven us, and we are called to forgive others. When it seems impossible to forgive, we call on God's grace to work in us and through us to bring peace to our relationships, congregations, communities, and the world.

Prayer

Thank you, God, for forgiving us. Let your love and forgiveness flow through us to others. Amen.

Colossians 3:16-17

Let the word of Christ dwell in you richly; teach and admonish one another in all wisdom; and with gratitude in your hearts sing psalms, hymns, and spiritual songs to God. And whatever you do, in word or deed, do everything in the name of the Lord Jesus, giving thanks to God the Father through him.

To ponder

The song of rejoicing softens hard hearts.—Hildegard von Bingen

Music

Music reflects our emotions—gratefulness, sorrow, fear, love, longing. Music is a gift from our loving God that can provide us with comfort, joy, and hope, whether we make music ourselves or listen to music made by others.

I take part in a pharmaceutical study designed to determine the effectiveness of a new drug to prevent Alzheimer's disease. I am eligible for the study because I have a family history, but I show no symptoms of the disease even though I am of an age to do so. There are monthly IV infusions of the drug, significant blood draws, hours of cognitive testing, physicals, and magnetic resonance imaging (MRI) of the brain. What I dread most is the MRI. Every six months I must slide into the "tube," remain motionless, hear loud banging sounds, see strange lights, and sense odd vibrations for twenty minutes. The technician offers headphones and music, but instead I silently "sing" hymns of comfort, joy, love, and peace. Long before I get through my playlist, the procedure is over.

Thanks be to God for music to soothe, inspire, encourage, and free us from fear! Music can help us hear God speak and can remind us that the Spirit is present in our lives, right beside us always, now and forever!

Prayer

Thank you, God, for the blessed gift of music. Amen.

Psalm 148:1-4

Hallelujah! Praise the LORD from the heavens;
praise God in the heights.
Praise the LORD, all you angels;
sing praise, all you hosts of heaven.
Praise the LORD, sun and moon;
sing praise, all you shining stars.
Praise the LORD, heaven of heavens,
and you waters above the heavens.

To ponder

Though the billions of people on Earth may come from different areas, we share a common heritage: we are all made of stardust! From the carbon in our DNA to the calcium in our bones, nearly all of the elements in our bodies were forged in the fiery hearts and death throes of stars.—"You Are Made of Stardust," NASA blog

The dance of the universe

The cosmos gives glory to God in explosive, creative, violent, silent, orderly, and chaotic worship! In massive nuclear fusion reactors (stars) that literally make the necessary components of everything we know, the heavens glow in praise to God. Through the majestic twirling of celestial bodies held together by powerful attraction (like galaxies and solar systems), the universe dances to the tune of God's endless song. In magificient supernovas, the vacuum of space is painted in dazzling fashion by nebula of endless potential that display God's ineffable splendor. In endless cycles of cataclysms and creation—endings and beginnings that have been happening for billions of years—the heavens proclaim the good news of life after death.

Spend a few moments in silence as you look up at the night sky or view amazing pictures from the James Webb Space Telescope (https://webb.nasa.gov). Allow yourself to be immersed in awe and wonder. Give thanks and praise to God!

Prayer

God of the universe, the heavens sing your praises. Give me a spirit of awe and wonder that inspires an endless song of thanks. Amen.

January 4

Psalm 148:7-9, 12
Praise the Lord from the earth,
you sea monsters and all deeps;
fire and hail, snow and fog,
tempestuous wind, doing God's will;
mountains and all hills,
fruit trees and all cedars; . . .
young men and maidens,
old and young together.

To ponder

All creation sings in wonder; even rocks and trees rejoice.
—"Earth Is Full of Wit and Wisdom," ACS 1064

All creation sings

All creation gives praise to God: fire by burning, wind by blowing, the deep by mystifying, fruit trees by feeding, mountains by standing tall, and even mosquitoes by buzzing around us! In a world of constant demands and instant gratification, it's difficult to slow down enough to experience the worship happening all around us. But whether we pay attention or not, it is happening—constantly. Animals and plants, rocks and soil, sand and water, germ and microbe are giving witness to God the creator and animator. We can join the praise of all the earth by opening our hearts and minds to the wonder of all that God has made.

And yet, our presence often inhibits that praise. Pollution of all kinds (air, water, light, ground, sound) threatens the delicate balance of our crucible of life. As we begin a new year, let us strive to bring our relationship with God's creation back into harmony. May all people, in all our beautiful diversity, join with creation and praise the Lord!

Prayer

God of all creation, enable us to perceive the hymn of praise that surrounds us every day, then turn us around to live in such a way that we join this chorus song. Amen.

Matthew 2:1-2

In the time of King Herod, after Jesus was born in Bethlehem of Judea, wise men from the East came to Jerusalem, asking, "Where is the child who has been born king of the Jews? For we observed his star at its rising, and have come to pay him homage."

To ponder

To worship God in Spirit and truth means to rightfully view God as a mighty force for justice. . . . To worship God in Spirit brings discomfort. To worship God is to offer our bodies as a living sacrifice, holy and pleasing to him (Rom. 12:1). . . . The time is now for the true worshipers to persist in the fight for justice individually and institutionally, in churches and communities.—Sheila Caldwell, "True Worship Means Real Justice"

Worship and working for justice

How we come before Jesus in worship matters, and we do this in various ways. King Herod said he wanted to find Jesus in order to worship him, but in reality, Herod wanted to neutralize a threat to his power. The magi from afar may have been eastern spiritual leaders, Zoroastrians, coming to celebrate the inbreaking of a benevolent God, or they may have been political envoys from the Nabataean Kingdom, a nation that opposed Rome, bringing gifts to make an alliance with the newborn king. Even today, some people worship Jesus seeking power, privilege, and riches, while others worship Jesus seeking transformation, liberation, justice, and love.

Think about why you and your faith community come to Jesus in worship. Are you looking for easy answers or engaging questions? Are you ready to give your life to Jesus so the Holy Spirit can show you the way to abundant life?

Prayer

Jesus, you come to us in a manger. As we come before you in worship, give us open minds, hearts, and wills to participate in your work of bringing justice, love, and peace to all. Amen.

Matthew 2:9-11

[The wise men] set out; and there, ahead of them, went the star that they had seen at its rising, until it stopped over the place where the child was. When they saw that the star had stopped, they were overwhelmed with joy. On entering the house, they saw the child with Mary his mother; and they knelt down and paid him homage. Then, opening their treasure chests, they offered him gifts of gold, frankincense, and myrrh.

To ponder

We should come to worship expecting to be changed. We are touching, tasting, feeling, hearing and seeing the one who knows us and loves us completely. Our lives are restored. We are set free. Fed for the journey we are set loose to go in peace and serve the Lord. Thanks be to God.—Elizabeth Eaton, "Worship Is the Heart of All We Do"

Bringing gifts to Jesus

The first response to the news of Jesus' birth is worship. Angels gather before the shepherds and sing their song of praise. Shepherds glorify and praise God after finding the newborn in a manger. Now the magi come with gifts to worship the child king.

Worship was my first love. As soon as I could speak the Lord's Prayer out loud, I led the congregation in prayer during worship. I found solace in leading worship, even in my adolescent years of deep doubt and searching. Worship connected me to friends, family, and a worldwide community. During a service of prayer around the cross, the walls in my heart came tumbling down and the good news of Jesus' presence with me became real. With tears running down my cheeks, I realized that all along, Jesus had been filling me with love, hope, joy, curiosity, and a thirst for justice. I was now ready to bring my gifts before Jesus in worship. What about you? What gifts will you bring to Jesus in this new year?

Prayer

Lord Jesus Christ, help us to perceive you at work in our lives, give us hearts for worship, and lead us to use our gifts in sharing your good news with all. Amen.

Household Blessings and Prayers

Advent

In the days of Advent, Christians prepare to celebrate the presence of God's Word among us in our own day. During these four weeks, we pray that the reign of God, which Jesus preached and lived, would come among us. We pray that God's justice would flourish in our land, that the people of the earth would live in peace, that the weak and the sick and the hungry would be strengthened, healed, and fed with God's merciful presence.

During the last days of Advent, Christians welcome Christ with names inspired by the prophets: wisdom, liberator of slaves, mighty power, radiant dawn and sun of justice, the keystone of the arch of humanity, and Emmanuel—God with us.

The Advent wreath

One of the best-known customs for the season is the Advent wreath. The wreath and winter candle-lighting in the midst of growing darkness strengthen some of the Advent images found in the Bible. The unbroken circle of greens is clearly an image of everlasting life, a victory wreath, the crown of Christ, or the wheel of time itself. Christians use the wreath as a sign that Christ reaches into our time to lead us to the light of everlasting life. The four candles mark the progress of the four weeks of Advent and the growth of light. Sometimes the wreath is embellished with natural dried flowers or fruit. Its evergreen branches lead the household and the congregation to the evergreen Christmas tree. In many homes, the family gathers for prayer around the wreath.

An evening service of light for Advent

This brief order may be used on any evening during the season of Advent. If the household has an Advent wreath (one candle for each of the four weeks of Advent), it may be lighted during this service. Alternatively, one simple candle (perhaps a votive candle) may be lighted instead.

Lighting the Advent wreath
May this candle/these candles be a sign of the coming light of Christ.
One or more candles may be lighted.

Week 1: Lighting the first candle

Blessed are you, God of Jacob, for you promise to transform weapons of war into implements of planting and harvest and to teach us your way of peace; you promise that our night of sin is far gone and that your day of salvation is dawning.

As we light the first Advent candle, wake us from our sleep, wrap us in your light, empower us to live honorably, and guide us along your path of peace.

O house of Jacob, come,
let us walk in the light of the Lord. Amen.

Week 2: Lighting the first two candles

Blessed are you, God of hope, for you promise to bring forth a shoot from the stump of Jesse who will bring justice to the poor, who will deliver the needy and crush the oppressor, who will stand as a signal of hope for all people.

As we light these candles, turn our wills to bear the fruit of repentance, transform our hearts to live in justice and harmony with one another, and fix our eyes on the shoot from Jesse, Jesus Christ, the hope of all nations.

O people of hope, come,
let us rejoice in the faithfulness of the Lord. Amen.

Week 3: Lighting three candles
Blessed are you, God of might and majesty, for you promise to make the desert rejoice and blossom, to watch over the strangers, and to set the prisoners free.

As we light these candles, satisfy our hunger with your good gifts, open our eyes to the great things you have done for us, and fill us with patience until the coming of the Lord Jesus.

O ransomed people of the Lord, come,
let us travel on God's holy way
and enter into Zion with singing. Amen.

Week 4: Lighting all four candles
Blessed are you, God of hosts, for you promised to send a Son, Emmanuel, who brought your presence among us; and you promise through your Son Jesus to save us from our sin.

As we light these candles, turn again to us in mercy; strengthen our faith in the word spoken by your prophets; restore us and give us life that we may be saved.

O house of David, come,
let us rejoice, for the Son of God, Emmanuel,
comes to be with us. Amen.

Reading
Read the scripture passage printed in the devotion for the day.

Hymn

One of the following hymns may be sung. The hymn might be accompanied by small finger cymbals.

"Light one candle to watch for Messiah," ELW 240
"People, look east," ELW 248
"Savior of the nations, come," ELW 263

During the final seven days of the Advent season (beginning December 17), the hymn "O come, O come, Emmanuel" (ELW 257) is particularly appropriate. The first stanza of the hymn could be sung each day during the final days before Christmas in addition to the stanza that is specifically appointed for the day.

First stanza
O come, O come, Emmanuel,
and ransom captive Israel,
that mourns in lonely exile here
until the Son of God appear.
Refrain Rejoice! Rejoice! Emmanuel shall come to you, O Israel.

December 17
O come, O Wisdom from on high,
embracing all things far and nigh:
in strength and beauty come and stay;
teach us your will and guide our way. *Refrain*

December 18

O come, O come, O Lord of might,
as to your tribes on Sinai's height
in ancient times you gave the law
in cloud, and majesty, and awe. *Refrain*

December 19

O come, O Branch of Jesse, free
your own from Satan's tyranny;
from depths of hell your people save,
and give them vict'ry o'er the grave. *Refrain*

December 20

O come, O Key of David, come,
and open wide our heav'nly home;
make safe the way that leads on high,
and close the path to misery. *Refrain*

December 21

O come, O Dayspring, come and cheer;
O Sun of justice, now draw near.
Disperse the gloomy clouds of night,
and death's dark shadow put to flight. *Refrain*

December 22

O come, O King of nations, come,
O Cornerstone that binds in one:
refresh the hearts that long for you;
restore the broken, make us new. *Refrain*

December 23

O come, O come, Emmanuel,
and ransom captive Israel,
that mourns in lonely exile here
until the Son of God appear. *Refrain*

Text: *Psalteriolum Cantionum Catholicarum*

Table prayer for Advent

Blessed are you, O Lord our God,
the one who is, who was, and who is to come.
At this table you fill us with good things.
May these gifts strengthen us
to share with the hungry and all those in need,
as we wait and watch for your coming among us
in Jesus Christ our Lord. Amen.

Christmas

Over the centuries, various customs have developed that focus the household on welcoming the light of Christ: the daily or weekly lighting of the Advent wreath, the blessing of the lighted Christmas tree, the candlelit procession of Las Posadas, the flickering lights of the luminaria, the Christ candle at Christmas.

The Christian household not only welcomes the light of Christ at Christmas but also celebrates the presence of that light throughout the Twelve Days, from Christmas until the Epiphany, January 6. In the Christmas season, Christians welcome the light of Christ that is already with us through faith. In word and gesture, prayer and song, in the many customs of diverse cultures, Christians celebrate this life-giving Word and ask that it dwell more deeply in the rhythm of daily life.

Lighting the Christmas tree

Use this prayer when you first illumine the tree or when you gather at the tree.

Holy God,
we praise you as we light this tree.
It gives light to this place
as you shine light into darkness through Jesus,
the light of the world.
God of all,

we thank you for your love,
the love that has come to us in Jesus.
Be with us now as we remember that gift of love,
and help us to share that love with a yearning world.
Creator God,
you made the stars in the heavens.
Thank you for the light that shines on us in Jesus,
the bright morning star.
Amen.

Blessing of the nativity scene
This blessing may be used when figures are added to the nativity scene and throughout the days of Christmas.

Bless us, O God, as we remember a humble birth. With each angel and shepherd we place here before you, show us the wonder found in a stable. In song and prayer, silence and awe, we adore your gift of love, Christ Jesus our Savior. Amen.

Table prayer for the twelve days of Christmas (December 25–January 5)
With joy and gladness we feast upon your love, O God.
You have come among us in Jesus, your Son,
and your presence now graces this table.
May Christ dwell in us
that we might bear his love to all the world,
for he is Lord forever and ever. Amen.

Epiphany

On the Epiphany of Our Lord (January 6), the household joins the church throughout the world in celebrating the manifestation, the "epiphany," of Christ to the world. The festival of Christmas is thus set within the context of outreach to the larger community; it possesses an outward movement. The festival of the Epiphany asks the Christian household: How might our faith in Christ the Light be shared with friends and family, with our neighbors, with the poor and needy in our land, with those who live in other nations?

Blessing for a home

Matthew writes that when the magi saw the shining star stop over-head, they were filled with joy. "On entering the house, they saw the child with Mary his mother" (Matthew 2:11). In the home, Christ is met in family and friends, in visitors and strangers. In the home, faith is shared, nurtured, and put into action. In the home, Christ is welcome.

Twelfth Night (January 5), Epiphany of Our Lord (January 6), or another day during the time after Epiphany offers an occasion for gathering with friends and family members for a blessing of the home. Someone may lead the greeting and blessing, while another person may read the scripture passage. Following an Eastern European tradition, a visual blessing may be inscribed with white chalk above the main door; for example, 20 + CMB + 25. The numbers change with each new year. The three letters stand for either the ancient Latin blessing Christe mansionem benedicat, *which means "Christ, bless this house," or the legendary names of the magi (Caspar, Melchior, and Balthasar).*

Greeting
Peace to this house and to all who enter here.
By wisdom a house is built,
and through understanding it is established;
through knowledge its rooms are filled
with rare and beautiful treasures. *(Proverbs 24:3-4)*

Reading
As we prepare to ask God's blessing on this household,
let us listen to the words of scripture.
In the beginning was the Word,
and the Word was with God, and the Word was God.
He was in the beginning with God.
All things came into being through him,
and without him not one thing came into being.
What has come into being in him was life,
and the life was the light of all people.
The Word became flesh and lived among us, and we have seen his glory,
the glory as of a father's only son, full of grace and truth.
From his fullness we have all received grace upon grace.
(John 1:1-4, 14, 16)

Inscription

This inscription may be made with chalk above the entrance:

20 + C M B + 25

Write the appropriate character (left) while speaking the text (right).

The magi of old, known as

C   Caspar,

M   Melchior, and

B   Balthasar,

followed the star of God's Son who came to dwell among us

20   two thousand

25   and twenty-five years ago.

+   Christ, bless this house,

+   and remain with us throughout the new year.

Prayer of Blessing

O God,

you revealed your Son to all people by the shining light of a star.

We pray that you bless this home and all who live here with your gracious presence.

May your love be our inspiration, your wisdom our guide, your truth our light, and your peace our benediction; through Christ our Lord. Amen.

Then everyone may walk from room to room, blessing the house with incense or by sprinkling with water, perhaps using a branch from the Christmas tree.

Table prayer for Epiphany

Generous God,
you have made yourself known in Jesus, the light of the world.
As this food and drink give us refreshment,
so strengthen us by your spirit,
that as your baptized sons and daughters
we may share your light with all the world.
Grant this through Christ our Lord.
Amen.

Notes

December 1: Text: German carol, 15th cent.; tr. Theodore Baker, 1851–1934; st. 1; "Lo, How a Rose E'er Blooming," ELW 272, st. 1. **December 2:** Robert Moor, *On Trails* (New York: Simon & Schuster, 2016). **December 3:** *Love Actually*, directed by Richard Curtis (Universal City, 2003). **December 4:** Colin Ellard, "Look Up: The Surprising Joy of Raising Your Gaze," *Psychology Today*, July 29, 2016, www.psychologytoday.com/us/blog/mind-wandering/201607 /look-the-surprising-joy-raising-your-gaze. **December 5:** Henri-Frédéric Amiel, *Amiel's Journal*, tr. Mary A. Ward, www.gutenberg.org /files/8545/8545-h/8545-h.htm. **December 6:** Text: Henry F. Lyte, 1793–1847; "Abide with Me," ELW 629, st. 2. **December 7:** John Krasinski, *Some Good News*, episode 1 (YouTube), https://youtu.be/ F5pgG1M_h_U?si=iiAr74KYkr2kumYY. **December 8:** Kaitlin B. Curtice, *Living Resistance: An Indigenous Vision for Seeking Wholeness Every Day* (Grand Rapids, MI: Brazos Press), 12. **December 9:** Oprah Winfrey on Maya Angelou, in Caroline Wanga, "Chief to Chief: Learning Love," *Essence* 54, no. 4:49. **December 10:** Mary Oliver, "Yes! No!," in *White Pine: Poems and Prose Poems* (New York: Ecco, 1994), 8. **December 11:** Rabindranath Tagore, *Fireflies: A Collection of Proverbs, Aphorisms and Maxims* (Hubbardston, MA: Asphodel, 2014). **December 12:** Jean-Jacques Rousseau, source unknown. Phillips Brooks, 1835–1893, "O Little Town of Bethlehem," ELW 279, st. 4. **December 13:** Henri J. M. Nouwen, *Here and Now: Living in the Spirit* (New York: Crossroad, 1994), pp. 19, 20. **December 14:** Loki, in "Heart of the TVA," season 2, episode 4 (Disney+, October 26, 2023). **December 15:** Mother

Teresa, *No Greater Love* (Novato, CA: New World Library, 1997), 42. **December 16:** Malcolm Guite, "St. John the Baptist: 1 St. John's Eve," *Sounding the Seasons: Poetry for the Christian Year* (Norwich: Canterbury, 2012). Also available at https://malcolmguite.wordpress .com/2018/06/22/a-pair-of-sonnets-for-st-john-the-baptist-2/. Josephus, *Jewish Antiquities* 18.5.2, §116–119. **December 17:** Robert Lowry, 1826–1899, "My Life Flows On in Endless Song," ELW 763, refrain. Martin Luther, "Sermon on the Afternoon of Christmas Day" (1530), ed. and tr. John W. Doberstein and Helmut T. Lehmann, *Luther's Works* (Philadelphia: Muhlenberg, 1959), 51:216. **December 18:** James W. Johnson, 1871–1938, "Lift Every Voice and Sing," ELW 841, st. 3. Henri J. M. Nouwen, *The Wounded Healer: Ministry in Contemporary Society* (New York: Image, 1972), 48–49. **December 19:** Howard Thurman, in Gil Bailie, *Violence Unveiled: Humanity at the Crossroads* (New York: Crossroads Publishing, 1995), xv. **December 20:** Sandra Cisneros, "*Tenemos* Layaway, or, How I Became an Art Collector," *A House of My Own: Stories from My Life* (New York: Alfred A. Knopf, 2015), 167. **December 21:** Text: John Helgen, b. 1957; © 2013 Augsburg Fortress, ACS 905. **December 22:** Meister Eckhart, *Meister Eckhart's Book of Darkness and Light: Meditations on the Path of the Wayless Way*, tr. Jon M. Sweeney, Mark S. Burrows, et al. (Newburyport, MA: Hampton Roads, 2023), 73. **December 23:** Mike Ramsdell, *A Train to Potevka* (Layton, UT: Zhivago, 2005). **December 24:** Text: Ken Bible, b. 1950; ©1996 Integrity's Hosanna! Music; "Love Has Come," ELW 292, st. 3. **December 25:** Text: Paul Gerhardt, 1607–1676; tr. composite; © 1930, 2006 Augsburg Fortress; "Evening and Morning," ELW

761, st. 1. **December 26:** Martin Luther, "The Magnificat," in *The Annotated Luther, Volume 4: Pastoral Writings*, ed. Mary Jane Haemig (Minneapolis: Fortress, 2016), 318. **December 27:** Mary Oliver, "Poem 102: When Death Comes," *New and Selected Poems: Volume 1* (Boston: Beacon, 1992). Library of Congress website accessed January 24, 2024: www.loc.gov/programs/poetry-and-literature /poet-laureate/poet-laureate-projects/poetry-180/all-poems/item /poetry-180-102/when-death-comes/?loclr=blogloc. **December 28:** Bryan Stevenson, *Just Mercy* (New York: One World, 2015), 290. **December 29:** Abraham Joshua Heschel, *Man Is Not Alone* (New York: Farrar, Straus & Giroux, 1976). **December 30:** Text: John Jacob Niles, 1892–1980; based on a traditional Appalachian carol, "I Wonder as I Wander," sts. 1–2. **January 1:** Joretta L. Marshall, *How Can I Forgive?* (Nashville: Abingdon, 2005). **January 2:** Hildegard von Bingen, *Scivias*, Book Three. **January 3:** "You Are Made of Stardust," NASA blog, July 1, 2022, https://nasa.tumblr.com/post /688583969233682432/you-are-made-of-stardust. **January 4:** Text: Adam M. L. Tice, b. 1979; © 2009 GIA Publications, Inc., "Earth Is Full of Wit and Wisdom," ACS 1064. **January 5:** Sheila Caldwell, "True Worship Means Real Justice," *Christianity Today*, August 14, 2020, www.christianitytoday.com/ct/2020/august-web-only /true-worship-means-real-justice.html. **January 6:** Elizabeth Eaton, "Worship Is the Heart of All We Do," *Living Lutheran*, April 20, 2015, www.livinglutheran.org/2015/04/worship-heart/.